DANTE

By T. S. Eliot

verse
COLLECTED POEMS, 1909–1962
FOUR QUARTETS
THE CULTIVATION OF CHRISTMAS TREES

selected verse
SELECTED POEMS
THE WASTE LAND

children's verse
OLD POSSUM'S BOOK OF PRACTICAL CATS

plays
COLLECTED PLAYS
MURDER IN THE CATHEDRAL
THE FAMILY REUNION
THE COCKTAIL PARTY
THE CONFIDENTIAL CLERK
THE ELDER STATESMAN

literary criticism
SELECTED ESSAYS
THE USE OF POETRY and the
USE OF CRITICISM
TO CRITICIZE THE CRITIC
ON POETRY AND POETS
INTRODUCING JAMES JOYCE
ELIZABETHAN DRAMATISTS
DANTE

social criticism
THE IDEA OF A CHRISTIAN SOCIETY
NOTES TOWARDS THE DEFINITION OF CULTURE

philosophy
KNOWLEDGE AND EXPERIENCE
in the philosophy of F. H. Bradley

selected prose
SELECTED PROSE (with Penguin Books Ltd.)

film script
THE FILM OF MURDER IN THE CATHEDRAL

translation
ANABASIS a poem by St.-John Perse

DANTE

by

T. S. ELIOT

FABER AND FABER
24 Russell Square
London

First published in mcmxxix
Published in 'Selected Essays' mcmxxxii
First published in this edition mcmlxv
by Faber and Faber Limited
24 Russell Square London WC1
Printed in Great Britain
by R. MacLehose & Co Glasgow

I

THE *INFERNO*

In my own experience of the appreciation of poetry I have always found that the less I knew about the poet and his work, before I began to read it, the better. A quotation, a critical remark, an enthusiastic essay, may well be the accident that sets one to reading a particular author; but an elaborate preparation of historical and biographical knowledge has always been to me a barrier. I am not defending poor scholarship; and I admit that such experience, solidified into a maxim, would be very difficult to apply in the study of Latin and Greek. But with authors of one's own speech, and even with some of those of other modern languages, the procedure is possible. At least, it is better to be spurred to acquire scholarship because you enjoy the poetry, than to suppose that you enjoy the poetry because you have acquired the scholarship. I was passionately fond of certain French poetry long before I could have translated two verses of it correctly. With Dante the discrepancy between enjoyment and understanding was still wider.

I do not counsel anyone to postpone the study of Italian grammar until he has read Dante, but certainly there is an immense amount of knowledge which, until one has read some of his poetry with intense pleasure — that is, with as keen pleasure as one is capable of getting from any poetry — is positively undesirable. In saying this I am avoiding two possible extremes of criticism. One might say that understanding of the scheme, the philosophy, the concealed meanings, of Dante's verse was *essential* to appreciation; and on the other hand one might say that these things were quite irrelevant, that the poetry in his poems was one thing, which could be enjoyed by itself without studying a framework which had served the author in producing the poetry but could not serve the reader in enjoying it. The latter error is the more prevalent, and is probably the reason why many people's knowledge of the *Comedy* is limited to the *Inferno*, or even to certain passages in it. The enjoyment of the *Divine Comedy* is a continuous process. If you get nothing out of it at first, you probably never will; but if from your first deciphering of it there comes now and then some direct shock of poetic intensity, nothing but laziness can deaden the desire for fuller and fuller knowledge.

What is surprising about the poetry of Dante is that it is, in one sense, extremely easy to read. It is a test (a positive test, I do not assert that it is always valid negatively), that genuine poetry can communicate before it is understood. The impression can be verified on fuller knowledge; I have found with Dante and with several other poets in languages in which I was unskilled, that about such impressions there was nothing fanciful. They were not due, that is, to *mis*understanding the passage, or to reading into it something not there, or to accidental sentimental evocations out of my own past. The impression was new, and of, I believe, the objective 'poetic emotion'. There are more detailed reasons for this experience on the first reading of Dante, and for my saying that he is easy to read. I do not mean that he writes very simple Italian, for he does not; or that his content is simple or always simply expressed. It is often expressed with such a force of compression that the elucidation of three lines needs a paragraph, and their allusions a page of commentary. What I have in mind is that Dante is, in a sense to be defined (for the word means little by itself), the most *universal* of poets in the modern languages. That does not mean that he is 'the greatest', or that he is the most comprehensive — there is greater variety and detail in Shakespeare. Dante's universality is not solely a personal matter. The Italian language, and especially the Italian language in Dante's age, gains much by being the product of universal Latin. There is something much more *local* about the languages in which Shakespeare and Racine had to express themselves. This is not to say, either, that English and French are inferior, as vehicles of poetry, to Italian. But the Italian vernacular of the late Middle Ages was still very close to Latin, as literary expression, for the reason that the men, like Dante, who used it, were trained, in philosophy and all abstract subjects, in mediaeval Latin. Now mediaeval Latin is a very fine language; fine prose and fine verse were written in it; and it had the quality of a highly developed and literary Esperanto. When you read modern philosophy, in English, French, German, and Italian, you must be struck by national or racial differences of thought: modern languages *tend* to separate abstract thought (mathematics is now the only universal language); but mediaeval Latin tended to concentrate on what men of various races and lands could think together. Some of the character of this universal language seems to me to inhere in Dante's Florentine speech; and the localization ('Florentine' speech) seems if anything to emphasize the universality, because it cuts across the modern division of nationality. To enjoy any French or German poetry, I think one needs to have some sympathy with the French or German mind; Dante, none the less an Italian and a patriot, is first a European.

This difference, which is one of the reasons why Dante is 'easy to read', may be discussed in more particular manifestations. The style of Dante has a peculiar lucidity — a *poetic* as distinguished from an *intellectual* lucidity. The thought may be obscure, but the word is lucid, or rather translucent. In English poetry words have a kind of opacity which is part of their beauty. I do not mean that the beauty of English poetry is what is called mere 'verbal

10

beauty'. It is rather that words have associations, and the groups of words *in* association have associations, which is a kind of local self-consciousness, because they are the growth of a *particular* civilization; and the same thing is true of other modern languages. The Italian of Dante, though essentially the Italian of to-day, is not in this way a modern language. The culture of Dante was not of one European country but of Europe. I am aware, of course, of a directness of speech which Dante shares with other great poets of pre-Reformation and pre-Renaissance times, notably Chaucer and Villon. Undoubtedly there is something in common between the three, so much that I should expect an admirer of any one of them to be an admirer of the others; and undoubtedly there is an opacity, or inspissation of poetic style throughout Europe after the Renaissance. But the lucidity and universality of Dante are far beyond those qualities in Villon and Chaucer, though they are akin.

Dante is 'easier to read', for a foreigner who does not know Italian very well, for other reasons: but all related to this central reason, that in Dante's time Europe, with all its dissensions and dirtiness, was mentally more united than we can now conceive. It is not particularly the Treaty of Versailles that has separated nation from nation; nationalism was born long before; and the process of disintegration which for our generation culminates in that treaty began soon after Dante's time. One of the reasons

11

for Dante's 'easiness' is the following — but first I must make a digression.

I must explain why I have said that Dante is 'easy to read', instead of talking about his 'universality'. The latter word would have been much easier to use. But I do not wish to be thought to claim a universality for Dante which I deny to Shakespeare or Molière or Sophocles. Dante is no more 'universal' than Shakespeare : though I feel that we can come nearer to understanding Dante than a foreigner can come to understanding those others. Shakespeare, or even Sophocles, or even Racine and Molière, are dealing with what is as universally human as the material of Dante; but they had no choice but to deal with it in a more local way. As I have said, the Italian of Dante is very near in feeling to mediaeval Latin : and of the mediaeval philosophers whom Dante read, and who were read by learned men of his time, there were, for instance, St. Thomas who was an Italian, St. Thomas's predecessor Albertus, who was a German, Abelard who was French, and Hugh and Richard of St. Victor who were Scots. For the *medium* that Dante had to use compare the opening of the *Inferno* :

> *Nel mezzo del cammin di nostra vita*
> *mi ritrovai per una selva oscura,*
> *che la diritta via era smarrita.*

In the middle of the journey of our life I found myself in a dark wood, having lost the straight path.

with the lines with which Duncan is introduced to Macbeth's castle :

This castle hath a pleasant seat; the air
Nimbly and sweetly recommends itself
Unto our gentle senses.
This guest of summer
The temple-haunting martlet, does approve
By his loved masonry that the heaven's breath
Smells wooingly here: no jutty, frieze,
Buttress, nor coign of vantage, but this bird
Hath made his pendant bed and procreant cradle:
Where they most breed and haunt, I have observed
The air is delicate.

I do not at all pretend that we appreciate everything, even in one single line of Dante, that a cultivated Italian can appreciate. But I do maintain that more is lost in translating Shakespeare into Italian than in translating Dante into English. How can a foreigner find words to convey in his own language just that combination of intelligibility and remoteness that we get in many phrases of Shakespeare ?

I am not considering whether the language of Dante or Shakespeare is superior, for I cannot admit the question : I merely affirm that the differences are such as make Dante easier for a foreigner. Dante's advantages are not due to greater genius, but to the fact that he wrote when Europe was still more or less one. And even had Chaucer or Villon been exact contemporaries of Dante, they would still have been farther, linguistically as well as geographically, from the centre of Europe than Dante.

But the simplicity of Dante has another detailed reason. He not only thought in a way in which every man of his culture in the whole of Europe then thought, but he employed a method which was common and commonly understood throughout Europe. I do not intend, in this essay, to go into questions of disputed interpretations of Dante's allegory. What is important for my purpose is the fact that the allegorical method was a definite method not confined to Italy; and the fact, apparently paradoxical, that the allegorical method makes for simplicity and intelligibility. We incline to think of allegory as a tiresome cross-word puzzle. We decline to associate it with dull poems (at best, *The Romance of the Rose*), and in a great poem to ignore it as irrelevant. What we ignore is, in a case like Dante's, its particular effect towards lucidity of style.

I do not recommend, in first reading the first canto of the *Inferno*, worrying about the identity of the Leopard, the Lion, or the She-Wolf. It is really better, at the start, not to know or care what they do mean. What we should consider is not so much the meaning of the images, but the reverse process, that which led a man having an idea to express it in images. We have to consider the type of mind which by nature and *practice* tended to express itself in allegory : and, for a competent poet, allegory means *clear visual images*. And clear visual images are given much more intensity by having a meaning — we do not need to know what that meaning is, but in our awareness of the image we must be aware that the meaning is there too. Allegory is only one poetic method, but it is a method which has very great advantages.

Dante's is a *visual* imagination. It is a visual imagination in a different sense from that of a modern painter of still life : it is visual in the sense that he lived in an age in which men still saw visions. It was a psychological habit, the trick of which we have forgotten, but as good as any of our own. We have nothing but dreams, and we have forgotten that seeing visions — a practice now relegated to the aberrant and uneducated — was once a more significant, interesting, and disciplined kind of dreaming. We take it for granted that our dreams spring from below: possibly the quality of our dreams suffers in consequence.

All that I ask of the reader, at this point, is to clear his mind, if he can, of every prejudice against allegory, and to admit at least that it was not a device to enable the uninspired to write verses, but really a mental habit, which when raised to the point of genius can make a great poet as well as a great mystic or saint. And it is the allegory which makes it possible for the reader who is not even a good Italian scholar to enjoy Dante. Speech varies, but our eyes are all the same. And allegory was not a local Italian custom, but a universal European method.

Dante's attempt is to make us see what he saw. He therefore employs very simple language, and very few metaphors, for allegory and metaphor do not get on well together. And there is a peculiarity about his *comparisons* which is worth noticing in passing.

There is a well-known comparison or simile in the great XVth canto of the *Inferno*, which Matthew Arnold singled out, rightly, for high praise; which is characteristic of the way in which Dante employs these figures. He is speaking of the crowd in Hell who peered at him and his guide under a dim light:

> *e sì ver noi aguzzavan le ciglia,*
> *come vecchio sartor fa nella cruna.*

and sharpened their vision (knitted their brows) at us, like an old tailor peering at the eye of his needle.

The purpose of this type of simile is solely to make us *see more definitely* the scene which Dante has put before us in the preceding lines.

> *she looks like sleep,*
> *As she would catch another Antony*
> *In her strong toil of grace.*

The image of Shakespeare's is much more complicated than Dante's, and more complicated than it looks. It has the grammatical form of a kind of

16

simile (the 'as if' form), but of course 'catch in her toil' is a metaphor. But whereas the simile of Dante is merely to make you see more clearly how the people looked, and is explanatory, the figure of Shakespeare is expansive rather than intensive; its purpose is to *add* to what you see (either on the stage or in your imagination) a reminder of that fascination of Cleopatra which shaped her history and that of the world, and of that fascination being so strong that it prevails even in death. It is more elusive, and it is less possible to convey without close knowledge of the English language. Between men who could make such inventions as these there can be no question of greater or less. But as the whole poem of Dante is, if you like, one vast metaphor, there is hardly any place for metaphor in the detail of it.

There is all the more reason to acquaint oneself well with Dante's poem first part by part, even dwelling specially on the parts that one likes most at first, because we cannot extract the full significance of any part without knowing the whole. We cannot understand the inscription at Hell Gate :

> *Giustizia mosse il mio alto Fattore;*
> *fecemi la divina Potestate,*
> *la somma Sapienza e il primo Amore.*

Justice moved my high Maker; what made me were the divine Power, the supreme Wisdom, and the primal Love.

until we have ascended to the highest Heaven and returned. But we can understand the first Episode that strikes most readers, that of Paolo and Francesca, enough to be moved by it as much as by any poetry, on the first reading. It is introduced by two similes of the same explanatory nature as that which I have just quoted :

> *E come gli stornei ne portan l'ali,*
> *nel freddo tempo, a schiera larga e piena,*
> *così quel fiato gli spiriti mali;*

And as their wings bear along the starlings, at the cold season, in large full troop.

> *E come i gru van cantando lor lai*
> *facendo in aer di sè lunga riga;*
> *così vid' io venir, traendo guai,*
> *ombre portate dalla detta briga;*

And as the cranes go chanting their lays, making themselves a long streak in the air, so I saw the wailing shadows come, wailing, carried on the striving wind.

We can see and feel the situation of the two lost lovers, though we do not yet understand the meaning which Dante gives it. Taking such an episode by itself, we can get as much out of it as we get from the reading of a whole single play of Shakespeare. We do not understand Shakespeare from a single reading, and certainly not from a single play. There is a relation between the various plays of Shakespeare, taken in order; and it is a work of years to venture even one individual interpretation of the pattern in Shakespeare's carpet. It is not certain that Shakespeare himself knew what it was. It is perhaps a larger pattern than Dante's, but the pattern is less distinct. We can read with full comprehension the lines :

> *Noi leggevamo un giorno per diletto*
> *di Lancillotto, come amor lo strinse;*
> *soli eravamo e senza alcun sospetto.*
> *Per più fiate gli occhi ci sospinse*
> *quella lettura, e scolorocci il viso;*
> *ma solo un punto fu quel che ci vinse.*
> *Quando leggemmo il disiato riso*
> *esser baciato da cotanto amante,*
> *questi, che mai da me non fia diviso,*
> *La bocca mi baciò tutto tremante:*

One day, for pastime, we read of Lancelot, how love constrained him; we were alone, and without all suspicion. Several times that reading urged our eyes to meet, and changed the colour of our faces; but one moment alone it was that overcame us. When we read how the fond smile was kissed by such a lover, he, who shall never be divided from me, kissed my mouth all trembling.

When we come to fit the episode into its place in the whole *Comedy*, and see how this punishment is related to all other punishments and to purgations and rewards, we can appreciate better the subtle psychology of the simple line of Francesca :

19

> *se fosse amico il re dell' universo*

if the King of the Universe were our friend. . . .

or of the line

> *Amor, che a nullo amato amar perdona*

Love, which to no loved one permits excuse for loving. . . .

or indeed of the line already quoted :

> *questi, che mai da me non fia diviso*

he, who shall never be divided from me. . . .

Proceeding through the *Inferno* on a first reading, we get a succession of phantasmagoric but clear images, of images which are coherent, in that each reinforces the last; of glimpses of individuals made memorable by a perfect phrase, like that of the proud Farinata degli Uberti :

> *ed ei s' ergea col petto e colla fronte,*
> *come avesse lo inferno in gran dispitto.*

He rose upright with breast and countenance, as though he entertained great scorn of Hell.

and of particular longer episodes, which remain separately in the memory. I think that among those which impress themselves most at the first reading are the episode of Brunetto Latini (Canto XV), Ulysses (Canto XXVI), Bertrand de Born (Canto XXVIII), Adamo di Brescia (Canto XXX), and Ugolino (Canto XXXIII).

20

Although I think it would be a mistake to skip, and find it much better to await these episodes until we come to them in due course, they certainly remain in my memory as the parts of the *Inferno* which first convinced me, and especially the Brunetto and the Ulysses episodes, for which I was unprepared by quotation or allusion. And the two may well be put together: for the first is Dante's testimony of a loved master of arts, the second his reconstruction of a legendary figure of ancient epic; yet both have the quality of *surprise* which Poe declared to be essential to poetry. This *surprise*, at its highest, could by nothing be better illustrated than by the final lines with which Dante dismisses the damned master whom he loves and respects :

> *Poi si rivolse, e parve di coloro*
> *che corrono a Verona il drappo verde*
> *per la campagna; e parve di costoro*
> *quegli che vince e non colui che perde.*

Then he turned back, and seemed like one of those who run for the green cloth at Verona through the open field; and of them he seemed like him who wins, and not like him who loses.

One does not need to know anything about the race for the roll of green cloth, to be *hit* by these lines; and in making Brunetto, so fallen, *run like the winner*, a quality is given to the punishment which belongs only to the greatest poetry. So Ulysses, unseen in the hornèd wave of flame,

Lo maggior corno della fiamma antica
cominciò a crollarsi mormorando,
pur come quella cui vento affatica.
Indi la cima qua e là menando,
come fosse la lingua che parlasse,
gittò voce di fuori e disse: 'Quando
mi diparti' da Circe, che sottrasse
me più d'un anno là presso a Gaeta. . . .'

*The greater horn of the ancient flame began to shake
itself, murmuring, like a flame struggling against the
wind. Then moving to and fro the peak, as though it
were the tongue that spoke, threw forth a voice and
said: 'When I left Circe, who kept me more than a year
there near Gaeta. . . .'*

is a creature of the pure poetic imagination, apprehensible apart from place and time and the scheme
of the poem. The Ulysses episode may strike us
first as a kind of excursion, an irrelevance, a self-
indulgence on the part of Dante taking a holiday
from his Christian scheme. But when we know the
whole poem, we recognize how cunningly and
convincingly Dante has made to fit in real men, his
contemporaries, friends, and enemies, recent historical personages, legendary and Biblical figures
and figures of ancient fiction. He has been reproved
or smiled at for satisfying personal grudges by
putting in Hell men whom he knew and hated; but
these, as well as Ulysses, are transformed in the
whole; for the real and the unreal are all representa-

tive of types of sin, suffering, fault, and merit, and all become of the same reality and contemporary. The Ulysses episode is particularly 'readable', I think, because of its continuous straightforward narrative, and because to an English reader the comparison with Tennyson's poem — a perfect poem at that — is very instructive. It is worth while noticing the greatly superior degree of *simplification* of Dante's version. Tennyson, like most poets, like most even of those whom we can call great poets, has to get his effect with a certain amount of *forcing*. Thus the line about the sea which

moans round with many voices,

a true specimen of Tennyson-Virgilianism, is too *poetical* in comparison with Dante, to be the highest poetry. (Only Shakespeare can be so 'poetical' without giving any effect of overloading, or distracting us from the main issue:

Put up your bright swords or the dew will rust them.)

Ulysses and his shipmates pass through the pillars of Hercules, that 'narrow pass'

ov' Ercole segnò li suoi riguardi
acciò che l'uom più oltre non si metta.

where Hercules set his marks, so that man should pass no farther.

'O frati', dissi, 'che per cento milia
perigli siete giunti all' occidente,

*a questa tanto picciola vigilia
de' vostri sensi, ch'è del rimanente,
non vogliate negar l'esperienza
di retro al sol, del mondo sanza gente.
Considerate la vostra semenza,
fatti non foste a viver come bruti
ma per seguir virtute e conoscenza.'*

'O brothers!' I said, 'who through a hundred thousand dangers have reached the West, deny not, to this so brief vigil of your senses that remains, experience of the world without men that lies behind the sun. Consider your nature, you were made not to live like beasts, but to pursue virtue and knowledge.'

They fare forth until suddenly

*n'apparve una montagna bruna
per la distanza, e parvemi alta tanto
quanto veduta non n'aveva alcuna.
Noi ci allegrammo, e tosto tornò in pianto,
chè dalla nuova terra un turbo nacque,
e percosse del legno il primo canto.
Tre volte il fe' girar con tutte l'acque,
alla quarta levar la poppa in suso,
e la prora ire in giù, com' altrui piacque,
infin che il mar fu sopra noi richiuso.*

there appeared a mountain brown in the distance; and it seemed to me the highest that I had ever seen. We rejoiced, but soon our joy was turned to lamentation: for a *storm came up from the new land, and caught the stem of our ship. Three times it whirled her round with all the waters; the fourth time it heaved up the stern and drove her down at the head, as pleased Another; until the sea closed over us.*

The story of Ulysses, as told by Dante, reads like a straightforward piece of romance, a well-told seaman's yarn; Tennyson's Ulysses is primarily a very self-conscious poet. But Tennyson's poem is flat, it has only two dimensions; there is nothing more in it than what the average Englishman, with a feeling for verbal beauty, can see. We do not need, at first, to know what mountain the mountain was, or what the words mean *as pleased Another*, to feel that Dante's sense has further depths.

It is worth pointing out again how very right was Dante to introduce among his historical characters at least one character who even to him could hardly have been more than a fiction. For the *Inferno* is relieved from any question of pettiness or arbitrariness in Dante's selection of damned. It reminds us that Hell is not a place but a *state*; that man is damned or blessed in the creatures of his imagination as well as in men who have actually lived; and that Hell, though a state, is a state which can only be thought of, and perhaps only experienced, by the projection of sensory images; and that the resurrection of the body has perhaps a deeper meaning than we understand. But these are such thoughts as come only after many readings; they are not necessary for the first poetic enjoyment.

The experience of a poem is the experience both of a moment and of a lifetime. It is very much like our intenser experiences of other human beings. There is a first, or an early moment which is unique, of shock and surprise, even of terror (*Ego dominus tuus*); a moment which can never be forgotten, but which is never repeated integrally; and yet which would become destitute of significance if it did not survive in a larger whole of experience; which survives inside a deeper and a calmer feeling. The majority of poems one outgrows and outlives, as one outgrows and outlives the majority of human passions : Dante's is one of those which one can only just hope to grow up to at the end of life.

The last canto (XXXIV) is probably the most difficult on first reading. The vision of Satan may seem grotesque, especially if we have fixed in our minds the curly-haired Byronic hero of Milton; it is too like a Satan in a fresco in Siena. Certainly no more than the Divine Spirit can the Essence of Evil be confined in one form and place; and I confess that I tend to get from Dante the impression of a Devil suffering like the human damned souls; whereas I feel that the *kind* of suffering experienced by the Spirit of Evil should be represented as utterly different. I can only say that Dante made the best of a bad job. In putting Brutus, the noble Brutus, and Cassius with Judas Iscariot he will also disturb at first the English reader, for whom Brutus and Cassius must always be the Brutus and Cassius of Shakespeare : but if my justification of Ulysses is valid, then the presence of Brutus and Cassius is also. If anyone is repelled by the last canto of the *Inferno*, I can only ask him to wait until he has read and lived for years with the last canto of the *Paradiso*, which is to my thinking the highest point that poetry has ever reached or ever can reach, and in which Dante amply repairs any failure of Canto XXXIV of the *Inferno*; but perhaps it is better, on our first reading of the *Inferno*, to omit the last canto and return to the beginning of Canto III :

> *Per me si va nella città dolente;*
> *   per me si va nell' eterno dolore;*
> *   per me si va tra la perduta gente.*
> *Giustizia mosse il mio alto Fattore;*
> *   fecemi la divina Potestate,*
> *   la somma Sapienza e il primo Amore.*

II

THE *PURGATORIO* AND
THE *PARADISO*

For the science or art of writing verse, one has
learned from the *Inferno* that the greatest poetry
can be written with the greatest economy of words,
and with the greatest austerity in the use of metaphor, simile, verbal beauty, and elegance. When I
affirm that more can be learned about how to write
poetry from Dante than from any English poet, I do
not at all mean that Dante's way is the only right
way, or that Dante is thereby *greater* than Shakespeare or, indeed, any other English poet. I put my
meaning into other words by saying that Dante can
do less *harm* to anyone trying to learn to write verse,
than can Shakespeare. Most great English poets are
inimitable in a way in which Dante was not. If you
try to imitate Shakespeare you will certainly pro-
duce a series of stilted, forced, and violent distor-
tions of language. The language of each great
English poet is his own language; the language of
Dante is the perfection of a common language. In a
sense, it is more pedestrian than that of Dryden or
Pope. If you follow Dante without talent, you will
at worst be pedestrian and flat; if you follow

Shakespeare or Pope without talent, you will make an utter fool of yourself.

But if one has learned this much from the *Inferno*, there are other things to be learnt from the two successive divisions of the poem. From the *Purgatorio* one learns that a straightforward philosophical statement can be great poetry; from the *Paradiso*, that more and more rarefied and remote *states of beatitude* can be the material for great poetry. And gradually we come to admit that Shakespeare understands a greater extent and variety of human life than Dante; but that Dante understands deeper degrees of degradation and higher degrees of exaltation. And a further wisdom is reached when we see clearly that this indicates the equality of the two men.

On the other hand, the *Purgatorio* and the *Paradiso* belong, in the way of understanding, together. It is apparently easier to accept damnation as poetic material than purgation or beatitude; less is involved that is strange to the modern mind. I insist that the full meaning of the *Inferno* can only be extracted after appreciation of the two later parts, yet it has sufficient meaning in and by itself for the first few readings. Indeed, the *Purgatorio* is, I think, the most difficult of the three parts. It cannot be enjoyed by itself like the *Inferno*, nor can it be enjoyed merely as a sequel to the *Inferno*; it requires appreciation of the *Paradiso* as well; which means that its first reading is arduous and apparently unremunerative. Only when we have read straight through to the end of the *Paradiso*, and re-read the *Inferno*, does the *Purgatorio* begin to yield its beauty. Damnation and even blessedness are more exciting than purgation.

By compensation, the *Purgatorio* has a few episodes which, so to speak, 'let us up' (as the counterpart to letting down) more easily than the rest, from the *Inferno*. We must not stop to orient ourselves in the new astronomy of the Mount of Purgatory. We must linger first with the shades of Casella and Manfred slain, and especially Buonconte and La Pia, those whose souls were saved from Hell only at the last moment.

> '*Io fui di Montefeltro, io son Buonconte;*
> *Giovanna o altri non ha di me cura;*
> *per ch'io vo tra costor con bassa fronte*'.
> *Ed io a lui:* '*Qual forza o qual ventura*
> *ti traviò sì fuor di Campaldino*
> *che non si seppe mai tua sepoltura?*'
> '*Oh*', *rispos' egli,* '*a piè del Casentino*
> *traversa un' acqua che ha nome l'Archiano,*
> *che sopra l'Ermo nasce in Apennino.*
> *Dove il vocabol suo diventa vano*
> *arriva' io forato nella gola,*
> *fuggendo a piede e sanguinando il piano.*
> *Quivi perdei la vista, e la parola*
> *nel nome di Maria finii: e quivi*
> *caddi, e rimase la mia carne sola.*'

'*I was of Montefeltro, I am Buonconte; neither
Giovanna nor any other has care of me, wherefore I go
with these, with lowered brow.*' I said to him: '*What
force or chance led you so far away from Campaldino
that your place of sepulture has always been unknown?*'
'*Oh*', said he, '*at the foot of Casentino a stream crosses,
which is called Archiano, and rises in the Apennines
above the Hermitage. There, where its name is lost,
came I, jabbed in the throat, fleeing on foot, dripping
blood over the plain. There my sight left me, and I
ended speech with (crying on) the name of Mary.
There I fell, and my flesh alone remained.*'

When Buonconte ends his story, the third spirit
speaks :

> '*Deh, quando tu sarai tornato al mondo,*
>   *e riposato della lunga via,*'
>   *seguitò il terzo spirito al secondo,*
> '*ricorditi di me, che son la Pia;*
>   *Siena mi fe', disfecemi Maremma:*
>   *salsi colui che innanellata, pria*
> *disposando, m'avea con la sua gemma.*'

'*O pray, when you return to the world, and are rested
from your long journey,*' followed the third spirit after
the second, '*remember me, who am La Pia. Siena
made me, Maremma unmade me: this is known to him
who after due engagement wedded me with his ring.*'

The next episode that impresses the reader
coming fresh from the *Inferno* is the meeting with

Sordello the poet (Canto VI), the soul who appeared

> *altera e disdegnosa*
> *e nel mover degli occhi onesta e tarda!*

proud and disdainful, *superb and slow in the move-
ment of his eyes!*

> *E il dolce duca incominciava:*
> *'Mantova'. . . e l'ombra, tutta in sè romita,*
> *surse ver lui del loco ove pria stava,*
> *dicendo: 'O Mantovano, io son Sordello*
> *della tua terra.' E l'un l'altro abbracciava.*

*The gentle guide (Virgil) began: 'Mantua'. . . and
the shade, suddenly rapt, leapt towards him from the
place where first it was, saying: 'O Mantuan, I am
Sordello of thy very soil.' And the one embraced the
other.*

The meeting with Sordello *a guisa di leon quando
si posa,* like a couchant lion, is no more affecting
than that with the poet Statius, in Canto XXI.
Statius, when he recognizes his master Virgil,
stoops to clasp his feet, but Virgil answers — the
lost soul speaking to the saved :

>   *'Frate,*
> *non far, chè tu se' ombra, ed ombra vedi.'*
> *Ed ei surgendo: 'Or puoi la quantitate*
> *comprender dell' amor ch' a te mi scalda,*
> *quando dismento nostra vanitate,*
> *trattando l'ombre come cosa salda.'*

*'Brother! refrain, for you are but a shadow, and a
shadow is but what you see.' Then the other, rising:
'Now can you understand the quantity of love that
warms me towards you, so that I forget our vanity,
and treat the shadows like the solid thing.'*

The last 'episode' at all comparable to those of the
Inferno is the meeting with Dante's predecessors,
Guido Guinicelli and Arnaut Daniel (Canto XXVI).
In this canto the Lustful are purged in flame, yet we
see clearly how the flame of purgatory differs from
that of hell. In hell, the torment issues from the
very nature of the damned themselves, expresses
their essence; they writhe in the torment of their
own perpetually perverted nature. In purgatory the
torment of flame is deliberately and consciously
accepted by the penitent. When Dante approaches
with Virgil these souls in purgatory flame, they
crowd towards him:

> *Poi verso me, quanto potevan farsi,*
> *certi si feron, sempre con riguardo*
> *di non uscir dove non fossero arsi.*

*Then certain of them made towards me, so far as they
could, but ever watchful not to come so far that they
should* not be in the fire.

The souls in purgatory suffer because they *wish to
suffer*, for purgation. And observe that they suffer
more actively and keenly, being souls preparing for
blessedness, than Virgil suffers in eternal limbo. In

their suffering is hope, in the anaesthesia of Virgil is hopelessness; that is the difference. The canto ends with the superb verses of Arnaut Daniel in his Provençal tongue:

> *'Ieu sui Arnaut, que plor e vau cantan;*
> *consiros vei la passada folor,*
> *e vei jausen lo jorn, qu' esper, denan.*
> *Ara vos prec, per aquella valor*
> *que vos guida al som de l'escalina,*
> *sovegna vos a temps de ma dolor.'*
> POI S'ASCOSE NEL FOCO CHE GLI AFFINA.

'I am Arnold, who weeps and goes singing. I see in thought all the past folly. And I see with joy the day for which I hope, before me. And so I pray you, by that Virtue which leads you to the topmost of the stair — be mindful in due time of my pain.' Then dived he back into that fire which refines them.

These are the high episodes, to which the reader initiated by the *Inferno* must first cling, until he reaches the shore of Lethe, and Matilda, and the first sight of Beatrice. In the last cantos (XXIX–XXXIII) of the *Purgatorio* we are already in the world of the *Paradiso*.

But in between these episodes is the narrative of the ascent of the Mount, with meetings, visions, and philosophical expositions, all important, and all difficult for the uninstructed reader who finds it less exciting than the continuous phantasmagoria of the *Inferno*. The allegory in the *Inferno* was easy to swallow or ignore, because we could, so to speak, grasp the concrete end of it, its solidification into imagery; but as we ascend from Hell to Heaven we are more and more required to grasp the whole from idea to image.

Here I must make a diversion, before tackling a specifically philosophical passage of the *Purgatorio*, concerning the nature of Belief. I wish merely to indicate certain tentative conclusions of my own, which might affect one's reading of the *Purgatorio*.

Dante's debt to St. Thomas Aquinas, like his debt (a much smaller one) to Virgil, can be easily exaggerated; for it must not be forgotten that Dante read and made use of other great mediaeval philosophers as well. Nevertheless, the question of how much Dante took from Aquinas and how much from elsewhere is one which has been settled by others and is not relevant to my present essay. But the question of what Dante 'believed' is always relevant. It would not matter, if the world were divided between those persons who are capable of taking poetry simply for what it is and those who cannot take it at all; if so, there would be no need to talk about this question to the former and no use in talking about it to the latter. But most of us are somewhat impure and apt to confuse issues : hence the justification of writing books about books, in the hope of straightening things out.

My point is that you cannot afford to *ignore* Dante's philosophical and theological beliefs, or to skip the passages which express them most clearly; but that on the other hand you are not called upon to believe them yourself. It is wrong to think that there are parts of the *Divine Comedy* which are of interest only to Catholics or to mediaevalists. For there is a difference (which here I hardly do more than assert) between philosophical *belief* and poetic *assent*. I am not sure that there is not as great a difference between philosophical belief and scientific belief; but that is a difference only now beginning to appear, and certainly inapposite to the thirteenth century. In reading Dante you must enter the world of thirteenth-century Catholicism, which is not the world of modern Catholicism, as his world of physics is not the world of modern physics. You are not called upon to believe what Dante believed, for your belief will not give you a groat's worth more of understanding and appreciation; but you are called upon more and more to understand it. If you can read poetry as poetry, you will 'believe' in Dante's theology exactly as you believe in the physical reality of his journey; that is, you suspend both belief and disbelief. I will not deny that it may be in practice easier for a Catholic to grasp the meaning, in many places, than for the ordinary agnostic; but that is not because the Catholic believes, but because he has been instructed. It is a matter of knowledge and ignorance, not of belief or scepticism. The vital matter is that Dante's poem is a whole; that you must in the end

come to understand every part in order to understand any part.

Furthermore, we can make a distinction between
what Dante believes as a poet and what he believed
as a man. Practically, it is hardly likely that even so
great a poet as Dante could have composed the
Comedy merely with understanding and without
belief; but his private belief becomes a different
thing in becoming poetry. It is interesting to
hazard the suggestion that this is truer of Dante
than of any other philosophical poet. With Goethe,
for instance, I often feel too acutely 'this is what
Goethe the man believed', instead of merely enter-
ing into a world which Goethe has created; with
Lucretius also; less with the *Bhagavad-Gita*, which
is the next greatest philosophical poem to the
Divine Comedy within my experience. That is the
advantage of a coherent traditional system of dogma
and morals like the Catholic: it stands apart, for
understanding and assent even without belief, from
the single individual who propounds it. Goethe
always arouses in me a strong sentiment of disbelief in what he believes: Dante does not. I believe
that this is because Dante is the purer poet, not
because I have more sympathy with Dante the man
than Goethe the man.

We are not to take Dante for Aquinas or
Aquinas for Dante. It would be a grievous error in
psychology. The *belief attitude* of a man reading the
Summa must be different from that of a man reading

Dante, even when it is the same man, and that man a Catholic.

It is not necessary to have read the *Summa* (which usually means, in practice, reading some handbook) in order to understand Dante. But it is necessary to read the philosophical passages of Dante with the humility of a person visiting a new world, who admits that every part is essential to the whole. What is necessary to appreciate the poetry of the *Purgatorio* is not belief, but suspension of belief. Just as much effort is required of any modern person to accept Dante's allegorical method, as is required of the agnostic to accept his theology.

When I speak of understanding, I do not mean merely knowledge of books or words, any more than I mean belief: I mean a state of mind in which one sees certain beliefs, as the order of the deadly sins, in which treachery and pride are greater than lust, and despair the greatest, as *possible*, so that we suspend our judgment altogether.

In the XVIth Canto of the *Purgatorio* we meet Marco Lombardo, who discourses at some length on the Freedom of the Will, and on the Soul:

> *Esce di mano a lui, che la vagheggia*
> *prima che sia, a guisa di fanciulla*
> *che piangendo e ridendo pargoleggia,*
> *l'anima semplicetta, che sa nulla,*
> *salvo che, mossa da lieto fattore,*
> *volentier torna a ciò che la trastulla.*

Di picciol bene in pria sente sapore;
quivi s'inganna, e retro ad esso corre,
se guida o fren non torce suo amore.
Onde convenne legge per fren porre;
convenne rege aver, che discernesse
della vera cittade almen la torre.

From the hands of Him who loves her before she is,
there issues like a little child that plays, with weeping
and laughter, the simple soul, that knows nothing
except that, come from the hands of a glad creator, she
turns willingly to everything that delights her. First she
tastes the flavour of a trifling good; then she is beguiled,
and pursues it, if neither guide nor check withhold her.
Therefore laws were needed as a curb; a ruler was needed,
who should at least see afar the tower of the true City.

Later (Canto XVII) it is Virgil himself who in-
structs Dante in the nature of Love :

'Nè creator nè creatura mai,'
cominciò ei, 'figliuol, fu senza amore,
o naturale o d'animo; e tu il sai.
Lo natural è sempre senza errore,
ma l'altro puote errar per malo obbietto,
o per poco o per troppo di vigore.
Mentre ch'egli è ne' primi ben diretto,
e ne' secondi sè stesso misura,
esser non può cagion di mal diletto;
ma, quando al mal si torce, o con più cura
o con men che non dee corre nel bene,
contra il fattore adopra sua fattura.

Quinci comprender puoi ch'esser conviene
amor sementa in voi d'ogni virtute,
e d'ogni operazion che merta pene.'

*He began: 'Neither Creator, nor creature, my son, was
ever without love, either natural or rational: and you
know it. The natural is always without error; but the
other may err through mistaking the object, or through
excess or deficiency of force. While it is directed towards the primal goods, and in the secondary moderates
itself, it cannot be the cause of delight of sin; but when
it turns to evil, or hurries towards the good with more
or less solicitude than is right, then the creature works
against the Creator. Accordingly you may understand
how Love must be the seed in you both of every virtue
and of every act that merits punishment.'*

I have quoted these two passages at some length,
because they are of the sort that a reader might be
inclined to skip, thinking that they are only for
scholars, not for readers of poetry, or thinking that
it is necessary to have studied the philosophy under-
lying them. It is not necessary to have traced the
descent of this theory of the soul from Aristotle's
De Anima in order to appreciate it as poetry. Indeed,
if we worry too much about it at first as philosophy
we are likely to prevent ourselves from receiving
the poetic beauty. It is the philosophy of that world
of poetry which we have entered.

But with the XXVIIth canto we have left behind
the stage of punishment and the stage of dialectic,

and approach the state of Paradise. The last cantos have the quality of the *Paradiso* and prepare us for it; they move straight forward, with no detour or delay. The three poets, Virgil, Statius, and Dante, pass through the wall of flame which separates Purgatory from the Earthly Paradise. Virgil dismisses Dante, who henceforth shall proceed with a higher guide, saying

> *Non aspettar mio dir più, nè mio cenno.*
> *Libero, dritto e sano è tuo arbitrio,*
> *e fallo fora non fare a suo senno:*
> *per ch'io te sopra te corono e mitrio.*

No more expect my word, or sign. Your Will is free, straight and whole, and not to follow its direction would be sin: wherefore I crown and mitre you (king and bishop) over yourself.

I.e. Dante has now arrived at a condition, for the purposes of the rest of his journey, which is that of the blessed : for political and ecclesiastical organization are only required because of the imperfections of the human will. In the Earthly Paradise Dante encounters a lady named Matilda, whose identity need not at first bother us,

> *una donna soletta, che si gia*
> *cantando ed iscegliendo fior da fiore,*
> *ond' era pinta tutta la sua via.*

A lady alone, who went singing and plucking flower after flower, wherewith her path was pied.

41

After some conversation, and explanation by Matilda of the reason and nature of the place, there follows a 'Divine Pageant'. To those who dislike — not what are popularly called pageants — but the serious pageants of royalty, of the Church, of military funerals — the 'pageantry' which we find here and in the *Paradiso* will be tedious; and still more to those, if there be any, who are unmoved by the splendour of the Revelation of St. John. It belongs to the world of what I call the *high dream*, and the modern world seems capable only of the *low dream*. I arrived at accepting it, myself, only with some difficulty. There were at least two prejudices, one against Pre-Raphaelite imagery, which was natural to one of my generation, and perhaps affects generations younger than mine. The other prejudice — which affects this end of the *Purgatorio* and the whole of the *Paradiso* — is the prejudice that poetry not only must be found *through* suffering but can find its material only *in* suffering. Everything else was cheerfulness, optimism, and hopefulness; and these words stood for a great deal of what one hated in the nineteenth century. It took me many years to recognize that the states of improvement and beatitude which Dante describes are still further from what the modern world can conceive as cheerfulness, than are his states of damnation. And little things put one off: Rossetti's *Blessed Damozel*, first by my rapture and next by my revolt, held up my appreciation of Beatrice by many years.

We cannot understand fully Canto XXX of the *Purgatorio* until we know the *Vita Nuova*, which in my opinion should be read after the *Divine Comedy*. But at least we can begin to understand how skilfully Dante expresses the recrudescence of an ancient passion in a new emotion, in a new situation, which comprehends, enlarges, and gives a meaning to it.

> *Sopra candido vel cinta d'oliva*
> *donna m'apparve, sotto verde manto,*
> *vestita di color di fiamma viva.*
> *E lo spirito mio, che già cotanto*
> *tempo era stato che alla sua presenza*
> *non era di stupor, tremando, affranto,*
> *senza degli occhi aver più conoscenza,*
> *per occulta virtù che da lei mosse,*
> *d'antico amor sentì la gran potenza.*
> *Tosto che nella vista mi percosse*
> *l'alta virtù, che già m'avea trafitto*
> *prima ch'io fuor di puerizia fosse,*
> *volsimi alla sinistra col rispitto*
> *col quale il fantolin corre alla mamma,*
> *quando ha paura o quando egli è afflitto,*
> *per dicere a Virgilio: 'Men che dramma*
> *di sangue m' è rimaso, che non tremi;*
> *conosco i segni dell' antica fiamma.'*

Olive-crowned over a white veil, a lady appeared to me, clad, under a green mantle, in colour of living flame. And my spirit, after so many years since trembling in her presence it had been broken with awe, without further knowledge by my eyes, felt, through hidden power which went out from her, the great strength of the old love. As soon as that lofty power struck my sense, which already had transfixed me before my adolescence, I turned leftwards with the trust of the little child who runs to his mama when he is frightened or distressed, to say to Virgil: 'Hardly a drop of blood in my body does not shudder: I know the tokens of the ancient flame.'

And in the dialogue that follows we see the passionate conflict of the old feelings with the new; the effort and triumph of a new renunciation, greater than renunciation at the grave, because a renunciation of feelings that persist beyond the grave. In a way, these cantos are those of the greatest *personal* intensity in the whole poem. In the *Paradiso* Dante himself, save for the Cacciaguida episode, becomes de- or super-personalized; and it is in these last cantos of the *Purgatorio*, rather than in the *Paradiso*, that Beatrice appears most clearly. But the Beatrice theme is essential to the understanding of the whole, *not* because we need to know Dante's biography — not, for instance, as the Wesendonck history is supposed to cast light upon *Tristan* — but because of Dante's *philosophy* of it. This, however, concerns more our examination of the *Vita Nuova*.

The *Purgatorio* is the most difficult because it is the *transitional* canto: the *Inferno* is one thing, comparatively easy; the *Paradiso* is another thing, more difficult as a whole than the *Purgatorio*, because more a whole. Once we have got the hang of the kind of feeling in it no one part is difficult. The *Purgatorio*, here and there, might be called 'dry': the *Paradiso* is never dry, it is either incomprehensible or intensely exciting. With the exception of the episode of Cacciaguida — a pardonable exhibition of family and personal pride, because it provides splendid poetry — it is not episodic. All the other characters have the best credentials. At first, they seem less distinct than the earlier unblessed people; they seem ingeniously varied but fundamentally monotonous variations of insipid blessedness. It is a matter of gradual adjustment of our vision. We have (whether we know it or not) a prejudice against beatitude as material for poetry. The eighteenth and nineteenth centuries knew nothing of it; even Shelley, who knew Dante well and who towards the end of his life was beginning to profit by it, the one English poet of the nineteenth century who could even have begun to follow those footsteps, was able to enounce the proposition that our sweetest songs are those which tell of saddest thought. The early work of Dante might confirm Shelley; the *Paradiso* provides the counterpart, though a different counterpart from the philosophy of Browning.

The *Paradiso* is not monotonous. It is as various as any poem. And take the *Comedy* as a whole, you can compare it to nothing but the *entire* dramatic work of Shakespeare. The comparison of the *Vita Nuova* with the *Sonnets* is another, and interesting, occupation. Dante and Shakespeare divide the modern world between them; there is no third.

We should begin by thinking of Dante fixing his gaze on Beatrice:

> *Nel suo aspetto tal dentro mi fei,*
> *qual si fe' Glauco nel gustar dell' erba,*
> *che il fe' consorto in mar degli altri dei.*
> *Trasumanar significar per verba*
> *non si poria; pero l'esemplo basti*
> *a cui esperienza grazia serba.*

Gazing on her, so I became within, as did Glaucus, on tasting of the grass which made him sea-fellow of the other gods. To transcend humanity may not be told in words, wherefore let the instance suffice for him for whom that experience is reserved by Grace.

And as Beatrice says to Dante: '*You make yourself dull with false fancy*'; warns him, that here there are divers sorts of blessedness, as settled by Providence.

If this is not enough, Dante is informed by Piccarda (Canto III) in words which even those who know no Dante know:

> *In la sua voluntate è nostra pace.*

His will is our peace.

It is the mystery of the inequality, and of the indifference of that inequality, in blessedness, of the blessed. It is all the same, and yet each degree differs.

46

Shakespeare gives the greatest *width* of human passion; Dante the greatest altitude and greatest depth. They complement each other. It is futile to ask which undertook the more difficult job. But certainly the 'difficult passages' in the *Paradiso* are Dante's difficulties rather than ours : his difficulty in making us apprehend sensuously the various states and stages of blessedness. Thus the long oration of Beatrice about the Will (Canto IV) is really directed at making us *feel* the reality of the condition of Piccarda; Dante has to educate our senses as he goes along. The insistence throughout is upon states of feeling; the reasoning takes only its proper place as a means of reaching these states. We get constantly verses like

> *Beatrice mi guardò con gli occhi pieni*
> *di faville d'amor così divini,*
> *che, vinta, mia virtù diede le reni,*
> *e quasi mi perdei con gli occhi chini.*

Beatrice looked on me with eyes so divine filled with sparks of love, that my vanquished power turned away, and I became as lost, with downcast eyes.

The whole difficulty is in admitting that this is something that we are meant to feel, not merely decorative verbiage. Dante gives us every aid of images, as when

> *Come in peschiera, ch'è tranquilla e pura,*
> *traggonsi i pesci a ciò che vien di fuori*

> *per modo che lo stimin lor pastura;*
> *sì vid' io ben più di mille splendori*
> *trarsi ver noi, ed in ciascun s'udia:*
> Ecco chi crescerà li nostri amori.

As in a fishpond still and clear, the fishes draw near to anything that falls from without in such a way as to make them think it something to eat, so I saw more than a thousand splendours draw towards us, and in each was heard: Lo! here is one that shall increase our loves.

About the persons whom Dante meets in the several spheres, we need only to enquire enough to consider why Dante placed them where he did.

When we have grasped the strict *utility* of the minor images, such as the one given above, or even the simple comparison admired by Landor :

> *Quale allodetta che in aere si spazia*
> *prima cantando, e poi tace contenta*
> *dell' ultima dolcezza che la sazia,*

Like the lark which soars in the air, first singing, and then ceases, content with the last sweetness that sates her,

we may study with respect the more elaborate imagery, such as that of the figure of the Eagle composed by the spirits of the just, which extends from Canto XVIII onwards for some space. Such figures are not merely antiquated rhetorical devices, but serious and practical means of making the spiritual visible. An understanding of the rightness of such imagery is a preparation for apprehending the last and greatest canto, the most tenuous and most intense. Nowhere in poetry has experience so remote from ordinary experience been expressed so concretely, by a masterly use of that imagery of *light* which is the form of certain types of mystical experience.

> *Nel suo profondo vidi che s'interna,*
>   *legato con amore in un volume,*
>   *ciò che per l'universo si squaderna;*
> *sustanzia ed accidenti, e lor costume,*
>   *quasi conflati insieme per tal modo,*
>   *che ciò ch' io dico è un semplice lume.*
> *La forma universal di questo nodo*
>   *credo ch' io vidi, perchè più di largo,*
>   *dicendo questo, mi sento ch' io godo.*
> *Un punto solo m'è maggior letargo,*
>   *che venticinque secoli alla impresa,*
>   *che fe' Nettuno ammirar l'ombra d'Argo.*

Within its depths I saw ingathered, bound by love in one mass, the scattered leaves of the universe: substance and accidents and their relations, as though together fused, so that what I speak of is one simple flame. The universal form of this complex I think I saw, because, as I say this, more largely I feel myself rejoice. One single moment to me is more lethargy than twenty-five centuries upon the enterprise which made Neptune wonder at the shadow of the Argo (passing over him).

One can feel only awe at the power of the master

who could thus at every moment realize the in-apprehensible in visual images. And I do not know anywhere in poetry more authentic sign of great-ness than the power of association which could in the last line, when the poet is speaking of the Divine vision, yet introduce the Argo passing over the head of wondering Neptune. Such association is utterly different from that of Marino speaking in one breath of the beauty of the Magdalen and the opulence of Cleopatra (so that you are not quite sure what adjectives apply to which). It is the real right thing, the power of establishing relations between beauty of the most diverse sorts; it is the utmost power of the poet.

> *O quanto è corto il dire, e come fioco*
> *al mio concetto!*

How scant the speech, and how faint, for my con-ception!

In writing of the *Divine Comedy* I have tried to keep to a few very simple points of which I am convinced. First that the poetry of Dante is the one universal school of style for the writing of poetry in any language. There is much, naturally, which can profit only those who write Dante's own Tuscan language; but there is no poet in any tongue — not even in Latin or Greek — who stands so firmly as a model for all poets. I tried to illustrate his universal mastery in the use of images. In the actual writing I went so far as to say that he is safer to follow, even for us, than any English poet, including Shakespeare. My second point is that Dante's 'allegorical' method has great advantages for the writing of *poetry*: it simplifies the diction, and makes clear and precise the images. That in good allegory, like Dante's, it is not necessary to understand the meaning first to enjoy the poetry, but that our enjoyment of the poetry makes us want to understand the meaning. And the third point is that the *Divine Comedy* is a complete scale of the *depths* and *heights* of human emotion; that the *Purgatorio* and *Paradiso* are to be read as extensions of the ordinarily very limited human range. Every degree of the feeling of humanity, from lowest to highest, has, moreover, an intimate relation to the next above and below, and all fit together according to the logic of sensibility.

I have only now to make certain observations on the *Vita Nuova*, which may also amplify what I have suggested about the mediaeval mind expressed in allegory.

NOTE TO SECTION II

The theory of poetic belief and understanding here employed for a particular study is similar to that maintained by Mr. I. A. Richards (see his *Practical Criticism*, pp. 179 ff. and pp. 271 ff.) I say 'similar', because my own *general* theory is still embryonic, and Mr. Richards's also is capable of much further development. I cannot therefore tell how far the similarity extends; but for those who are interested in the subject, I should point out one respect in which my view differs from that of Mr. Richards; and then proceed to qualify my own tentative conclusions.

I am in agreement with Mr. Richards's statement on p. 271 (*op. cit.*). I agree for the reason that if you hold any contradictory theory you deny, I believe, the existence of 'literature' as well as of 'literary criticism'. We may raise the question whether 'literature' exists; but for certain purposes, such as the purpose of this essay on Dante, we must assume that there is literature and literary appreciation; we must assume that the reader can obtain the full 'literary' or (if you will) 'aesthetic' enjoyment without sharing the beliefs of the author. *If* there is 'literature', *if* there is 'poetry', then it must be possible to have full literary or poetic appreciation without sharing the beliefs of the poet. That is as far as my thesis goes in the present essay. It may be argued whether there is literature, whether there is poetry, and whether there is any meaning in the term 'full appreciation'. But I have assumed for this essay that these things exist and that these terms are understood.

I deny, in short, that the reader must share the beliefs of the poet in order to enjoy the poetry fully. I have also asserted that we can distinguish between Dante's beliefs as a man and his beliefs as a poet. But we are forced to believe that there is a particular relation between the two, and that the poet 'means what he says'. If we learned, for instance, that *De Rerum Natura* was a Latin exercise which Dante had composed for relaxation after completing the *Divine Comedy*, and published under the name of one Lucretius, I am sure that our capacity for enjoying either poem would be mutilated. Mr. Richards's statement (*Science and Poetry*, p. 76 footnote) that a certain writer has effected 'a complete severance between his poetry and *all* beliefs' is to me incomprehensible.

If you deny the theory that full poetic appreciation is possible without belief in what the poet believed, you deny the existence of 'poetry' as well as 'criticism'; and if you push this denial to its conclusion, you will be forced to admit that there is very little poetry that you can appreciate, and that your appreciation of it will be a function of your philosophy or theology or something else. If, on the other hand, I push *my* theory to the extreme, I find myself in as great a difficulty. I am quite aware of the ambiguity of the word 'understand'. In one sense, it means to understand without believing, for unless you can understand a view of life (let us say) without believing in it, the word 'understand' loses all meaning, and the act of choice between one view and another is reduced to caprice. But if you yourself are convinced of a certain view of life, then you irresistibly and inevitably believe that if anyone else comes to 'understand' it fully, his understanding *must* terminate in belief. It is possible, and sometimes necessary, to argue that full understanding must identify itself with full belief. A good deal, it thus turns out, hangs on the meaning, if any, of this short word *full*.

In short, both the view I have taken in this essay, and the view which contradicts it, are, if pushed to the end, what I call heresies (not, of course, in the theological, but in a more general sense). Each is true only within a limited field of discourse, but unless you limit fields of discourse, you can have no discourse at all. Orthodoxy can only be found in such contradictions, though it must be remembered that a pair of contradictions may *both* be false, and that not all pairs of contradictions make up a truth.

And I confess to considerable difficulty in analysing my own feelings, a difficulty which makes me hesitate to accept Mr. Richards's theory of 'pseudo-statements'. On reading the line which he uses,

> *Beauty is truth, truth beauty . . .*

I am at first inclined to agree with him, because this statement of equivalence means nothing to me. But on re-reading the whole Ode, this line strikes me as a serious blemish on a beautiful poem; and the reason must be either that I fail to understand it, or that it is a statement which is untrue. And I suppose that Keats meant something by it, however remote his truth and his beauty may have been from these words in ordinary use. And I am sure that he would have repudiated any explanation of the line which called it a pseudo-statement. On the other hand the line I have often quoted of Shakespeare,

Ripeness is all,

or the line I have quoted of Dante,

In la sua voluntate è nostra pace,

strikes very differently on my ear. I observe that the propositions in these words are very different in kind, not only from that of Keats, but from each other. The statement of Keats seems to me meaningless: or perhaps, the fact that it is grammatically meaningless conceals another meaning from me. The statement of Shakespeare seems to me to have profound emotional meaning, with, at least, no literal fallacy. And the statement of Dante seems to me *literally true*. And I confess that it has more beauty for me now, when my own experience has deepened its meaning, than it did when I first read it. So I can only conclude that I cannot, in practice, wholly separate my poetic appreciation from my personal beliefs. Also that the distinction between a statement and a pseudo-statement is not always, in particular instances, possible to establish. The theory of Mr. Richards is, I believe, incomplete until he defines the species of religious, philosophical, scientific, and other beliefs, as well as that of 'everyday' belief.

I have tried to make clear some of the difficulties inhering in my own theory. Actually, one probably has more pleasure in the poetry when one shares the beliefs of the poet. On the other hand there is a distinct pleasure in enjoying poetry as poetry when one does *not* share the beliefs, analogous to the pleasure of 'mastering' other men's philosophical systems. It would appear that 'literary appreciation' is an abstraction, and pure poetry a phantom; and that both in creation and enjoyment much always enters which is, from the point of view of 'Art', irrelevant.

III

THE *VITA NUOVA*

All of Dante's 'minor works' are important, because they are works of Dante; but the *Vita Nuova* has a special importance, because it does more than any of the others help us to a fuller understanding of the *Divine Comedy*. I do not suggest that the others may be neglected; the *Convivio* is important, and also the *De Volgari Eloquio*: and every part of Dante's writings can give us some light on other parts. But the *Vita Nuova* is a youthful work, in which some of the method and design, and explicitly the intention, of the *Divine Comedy*, are shown. Because it is an immature work, it requires some knowledge of the masterpiece to understand; and at the same time helps particularly towards understanding of the Comedy.

A great deal of scholarship has been directed upon examination of the early life of Dante, in connexion with the *Vita Nuova*. Critics may be roughly divided into those who regard it as primarily biographical, and those who regard it as primarily allegorical. It is much easier for the second group to make a good case than for the first. If this curious medley of verse and prose is biographical, then the biography has unquestionably been manipulated almost out of recognition to fit into conventional forms of allegory. The imagery of much of it is certainly in a very ancient tradition of vision literature : just as the scheme of the *Divine Comedy* has been shown to be closely similar to similar supernatural peregrination stories in Arabic and in old Persian literature — to say nothing of the descents of Ulysses and Æneas — so there are parallels to the visions of the *Vita Nuova* such as the *Shepherd of Hermas* in Greek. And as the book is obviously not a literal statement, whether of vision or delusion, it is easy to make out a case for its being an entire allegory : for asserting, that is, that Beatrice is merely a personification of an abstract virtue, intellectual or moral.

I wish to make clear that my own opinions are opinions founded only upon reading the text. I do not think that they are such as can either be verified or refuted by scholars; I mean to restrict my comments to the unprovable and the irrefutable.

It appears likely, to anyone who reads the *Vita Nuova* without prejudice, that it is a mixture of biography and allegory; but a mixture according to a recipe not available to the modern mind. When I say the 'modern mind', I mean the minds of those who have read or could have read such a document as Rousseau's *Confessions*. The modern mind can understand the 'confession', that is, the literal account of oneself, varying only in degree of sincerity and self-understanding, and it can understand 'allegory' in the abstract. Nowadays 'confessions', of an insignificant sort, pour from the press; everyone *met son cœur à nu*, or pretends to; 'personalities' succeed one another in interest. It is difficult to conceive of an age (of many ages) when human beings cared somewhat about the salvation of the 'soul', but not about each other as 'personalities'. Now Dante, I believe, had experiences which seemed to him of some importance; not of importance because they had happened to him and because he, Dante Alighieri, was an important person who kept press-cutting bureaux busy, but important in themselves; and therefore they seemed to him to have some philosophical and impersonal value. I find in it an account of a particular kind of experience : that is, of something which had actual experience (the experience of the 'confession' in the modern sense) *and* intellectual and imaginative experience (the experience of thought and the experience of dream) as its materials; and which became a third kind. It seems to me of importance to grasp the simple fact that the *Vita Nuova* is neither a 'confession' nor an 'indiscretion' in the modern sense, nor is it a piece of Pre-Raphaelite tapestry. If you have that sense of intellectual and spiritual realities that Dante had, then a form of expression like the *Vita Nuova* cannot be classed either as 'truth' or 'fiction'.

In the first place, the type of sexual experience

which Dante describes as occurring to him at the age of nine years is by no means impossible or unique. My only doubt (in which I found myself confirmed by a distinguished psychologist) is whether it could have taken place so *late* in life as the age of nine years. The psychologist agreed with me that it is more likely to occur at about five or six years of age. It is possible that Dante developed rather late, and it is also possible that he altered the dates to employ some other significance of the number nine. But to me it appears obvious that the *Vita Nuova* could only have been written around a personal experience. If so, the details do not matter : whether the lady was the Portinari or not, I do not care; it is quite as likely that she is a blind for someone else, even for a person whose name Dante may have forgotten or never known. But I cannot find it incredible that what has happened to others should have happened to Dante with much greater intensity.

The same experience, described in Freudian terms, would be instantly accepted as fact by the modern public. It is merely that Dante, quite reasonably, drew other conclusions and used another mode of expression, which arouses incredulity. And we are inclined to think — as Remy de Gourmont, for once misled by his prejudices into the pedantic attitude, thought — that if an author like Dante follows closely a form of vision that has a long history, it proves that the story is mere allegory (in the modern sense) or fake. I find a much greater difference in sensibility between the *Vita Nuova* and the *Shepherd of Hermas* than Gourmont did. It is not at all the simple difference between the genuine and the fraud; it is a difference in mind between the humble author of early Christian times and the poet of the thirteenth century, perhaps as great as that between the latter and ourselves. The similarities might prove that a certain *habit* in dream imagery can persist throughout many changes of civilization. Gourmont would say that Dante borrowed; but that is imputing our own mind to the thirteenth century. I merely suggest that possibly Dante, in his place and time, was following something more essential than merely a 'literary' tradition.

The attitude of Dante to the fundamental experience of the *Vita Nuova* can only be understood by accustoming ourselves to find meaning in *final causes* rather than in origins. It is not, I believe, meant as a description of what he *consciously* felt on his meeting with Beatrice, but rather as a description of what that meant on mature reflection upon it. The final cause is the attraction towards God. A great deal of sentiment has been spilt, especially in the eighteenth and nineteenth centuries, upon idealizing the reciprocal feelings of man and woman towards each other, which various realists have been irritated to denounce: this sentiment ignoring the fact that the love of man and woman (or for that matter of man and man) is only explained and made reasonable by the higher love, or else is simply the coupling of animals.

Let us entertain the theory that Dante, meditating on the astonishment of an experience at such an age, which no subsequent experience abolished or exceeded, found meanings in it which we should not be likely to find ourselves. His account is then just as reasonable as our own; and he is simply prolonging the experience in a different direction from that which we, with different mental habits and prejudices, are likely to take.

We cannot, as a matter of fact, understand the *Vita Nuova* without some saturation in the poetry of Dante's Italian contemporaries, or even in the poetry of his Provençal predecessors. Literary parallels are most important, but we must be on guard not to take them in a purely literary and literal way. Dante wrote more or less, at first, like other poets, not simply because he had read their works, but because his modes of feeling and thought were much like theirs. As for the Provençal poets, I have not the knowledge to read them at first hand. That mysterious people had a religion of their own which was thoroughly and painfully extinguished by the Inquisition; so that we hardly know more about them than about the Sumerians. I suspect that the difference between this unknown, and possibly maligned, Albigensianism and Catholicism has some correspondence with the difference between the poetry of the Provençal school and the Tuscan. The system of Dante's organization of sensibility — the contrast between higher and lower carnal love, the transition from Beatrice living to Beatrice dead, rising to the Cult of the Virgin, seems to me to be his own.

At any rate, the *Vita Nuova*, besides being a sequence of beautiful poems connected by a curious vision-literature prose is, I believe, a very sound psychological treatise on something related to what is now called 'sublimation'. There is also a practical sense of realities behind it, which is antiromantic : not to expect more from *life* than it can give or more from *human* beings than they can give; to look to *death* for what life cannot give. The *Vita Nuova* belongs to 'vision literature'; but its philosophy is the Catholic philosophy of disillusion.

Understanding of the book is greatly advanced by acquaintance with Guido Guinicelli, Cavalcanti, Cino, and others. One ought, indeed, to study the development of the art of love from the Provençal poets onwards, paying just attention to both resemblances and differences in spirit; as well as the development of verse form and stanza form and vocabulary. But such study is vain unless we have first made the conscious attempt, as difficult and hard as rebirth, to pass through the looking-glass into a world which is just as reasonable as our own. When we have done that, we begin to wonder whether the world of Dante is not both larger and more solid than our own. When we repeat

Tutti li miei penser parlan d'Amore

we must stop to think what *amore* means — something different from its Latin original, its French equivalent, or its definition in a modern Italian dictionary.

It is, I repeat, for several reasons necessary to read the *Divine Comedy* first. The first reading of the *Vita Nuova* gives nothing but Pre-Raphaelite quaintness. The *Comedy* initiates us into the world of mediaeval imagery, in the *Inferno* most apprehensible, in the *Paradiso* most rarefied. It initiates us also into the world of mediaeval thought and dogma : far easier for those who have had the college discipline of Plato and Aristotle, but possible even without that. The *Vita Nuova* plunges us direct into mediaeval sensibility. It is not, for Dante, a masterpiece, so that it is safer for us to read it, the first time, for the light it can throw on the *Comedy* than for itself.

Read in this way, it can be more useful than a dozen commentaries. The effect of many books about Dante is to give the impression that it is more necessary to read about him than to read what he has written. But the next step after reading Dante again and again should be to read some of the books that he read, rather than modern books about his work and life and times, however good. We may easily be distracted by following up the histories of

Emperors and Popes. With a poet like Shake-speare, we are less likely to ignore the text for the commentary. With Dante there is just as much need for concentrating on the text, and all the more because Dante's mind is more remote from the ways of thinking and feeling in which we have been brought up. What we need is not information but knowledge : the first step to knowledge is to recognize the differences between his form of thought and feeling and ours. Even to attach great importance to Thomism, or to Catholicism, may lead us astray, in attracting us too much to such differences as are entirely capable of intellectual formulation. The English reader needs to remember that even had Dante not been a good Catholic, even had he treated Aristotle or Thomas with sceptical indifference, his mind would still be no easier to understand; the forms of imagination, phantasmagoria, and sensibility would be just as strange to us. We have to learn to accept these forms : and this *acceptance* is more important than anything that can be called belief. There is almost a definite moment of acceptance at which the New Life begins.

What I have written is, as I promised, not an 'introduction' to the study but a brief account of my own introduction to it. In extenuation, it may be observed that to write in this way of men like Dante or Shakespeare is really less presumptuous than to write of smaller men. The very vastness of the subject leaves a possibility that one may have something to say worth saying; whereas with smaller men, only minute and special study is likely to justify writing about them at all.